Most of us want financial freedom, but starting a business sounds scary and risky, we even imagine it failing before it even begins!

Throughout the past 5 years I've built my social media platforms from 0 to over 600k+, and established my own international Cosmetics brand that's ranked better than 93% of similar businesses worldwide, resulting in over that 500k revenue in sales just last 6 months, and it all started from an Instagram business page, so let me share my experience with you and I can assure you that it won't fail as long as you keep working on it.

If you're already a business owner, having a professional Instagram page can really benefit you and add value to your business.

Maybe you want to start a business but you don't have enough money to spend on a shop or an office, can you start without a budget?

The obvious answer is Instagram or a Facebook page, but most people don't know what to do after they actually create the page, don't worry I will tell you how to build it, run it and grow it step by step.

What are the benefits of using Instagram for business?

- Increases Brand awareness.
- Increase website traffic and SEO rankings.
- Saves your time.
- Getting new customers at a low cost.
- Increase in sales.
- Provides you better audience insight.
- Gives a professional look to your clients.
- Legitimize your brand

  Customers tend to conduct online searches about the brand they like. If the same information is provided on social media, it helps a long way towards customer recognition of a brand's services and product, legitimizing it.

After choosing a business idea that suits your abilities & goes along with your passion, you can start building your brand or page.

Your page look is the first thing that your potential customers see, most businesses make a very common mistake by posting whatever they want, all the products they have mixed with offers or customers chats...etc. it looks very messy and unprofessional, but the good thing is that after reading this book you can leave the best impression possible for your customers.

You can start by choosing the right theme and colors for your business, for example, if the page is for a real estate agency you have to give a professional look with bold fonts and formal colors like black, grey, white, touch of gold …etc.

Or if the page is for a creative marketing services you can use bright attractive colors in your designs, so it depends on your business identity.

After putting that in mind, let's start!

1

Set up your profile

Now that you created an account, I know that this is very basic to say but it's an important point, you should setup your profile properly.

First, the main display picture should be your logo or your main product, on a white or a plain background.

After you've picked the right profile picture, make sure to fill the name bar as well. So why is that important? Well, your name and username are the only fields that Instagram considers in search queries which means you absolutely need to make sure that the name you use in your Instagram bio is the one your followers and customers are searching for!

Let's move to the bio box (the description), what can really improve your Insta-bio game are keywords which should be included in a way that makes you target audience find you and clearly understand your services.

It would be advisable to share your email or business number too. It makes it simple for your followers to contact you or customer care if they have any questions.

Example:

1,659 **32.6K** **1,236**
Posts Followers Following

Beauty By Retta©
Brand Based in UK 🇬🇧
.
#1 BEST SELLING Home IPL Laser 🏆
.
Colored Lenses, Modest Outfits,
Mink Lashes & More!
.
Owner @retta.a
Worldwide Delivery 🚚
www.beautybyretta.com

2

Create a logo

1-Choose the business name and create a professional logo, you can use "CANVA" (website and mobile application) this application will be your best friend throughout your business journey. Examples:

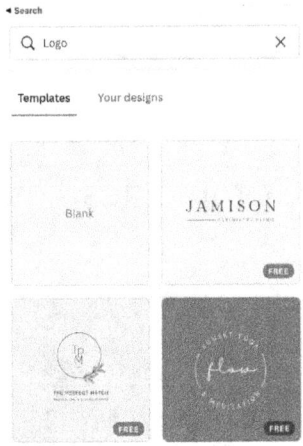

2

Graphic designs

2- Aesthetics is essential to be successful on Instagram. Choose your niche and stick to it. After designing your logo, you should create more designs using the same colors as the logo, talking about your products, services, prices, customer reviews or menu...etc.

Make sure all your photos have the same "vibe."

Tip: you can use the same filter on all pictures to give this look.

Example:

Services

- BOOK HOTELS
- RENT A CAR (LOW PRICES)
- PROFESSIONAL TOUR GUIDE
- DUBAI ACTIVITIES
- BEST SHOPPING PLACES
- DESERT SAFARI TRIPS
- YACHT TOURS

DUBAI TOURS

Contact us
+971082796161

DUBAI TOURS

LIVE THE BEST DUBAI EXPERIENCE

WITHOUT BREAKING YOUR BANK ACCOUNT!

Contact us
+971082796161

DUBAI TOURS

ENJOY YOUR TRIPS

WITH THE BEST DEALS

GET THE LOWEST PRICES!

Contact us
+971082796161

DUBAI TOURS

CUSTOMIZE A TRIP OF YOUR CHOICE !

Contact us
+971082796161

DUBAI TOURS

Services

- BOOK HOTELS
- RENT A CAR (LOW PRICES)
- PROFESSIONAL TOUR GUIDE
- DUBAI ACTIVITIES
- BEST SHOPPING PLACES
- DESERT SAFARI TRIPS
- YACHT TOURS

Contact us
+971082796161

DUBAI TOURS

ENJOY YOUR TRIPS

WITH THE BEST DEALS

GET THE LOWEST PRICES!

Contact us
+971082796161

DUBAI TOURS

CUSTOMIZE A TRIP OF YOUR CHOICE !

DUBAI TOURS

LIVE THE BEST DUBAI EXPERIENCE

WITHOUT BREAKING YOUR BANK ACCOUNT!

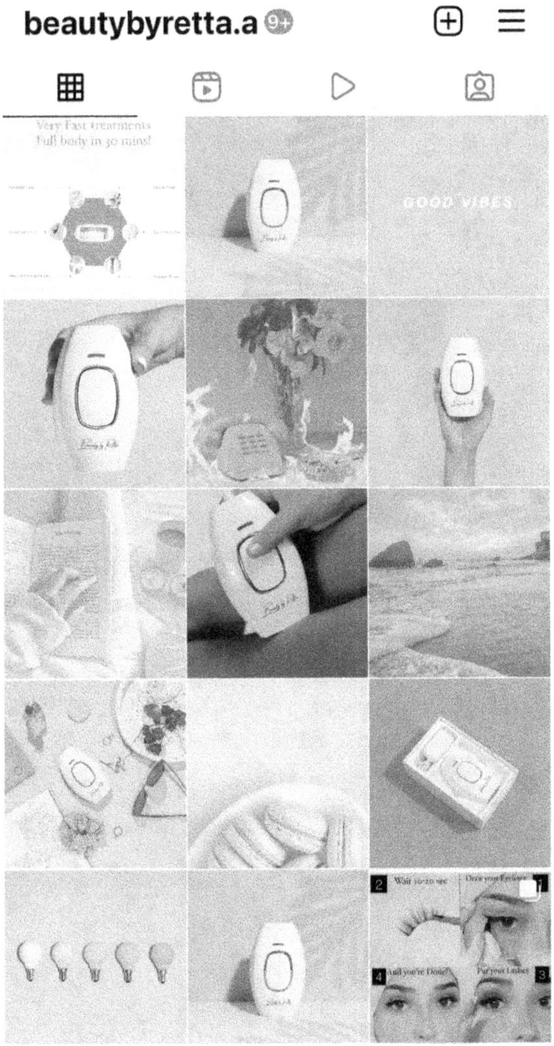
beautybyretta.a
Very Fast treatments
Full body in 30 mins!
GOOD VIBES

3

Main Caption

3- Now post those designs on the page with a clear caption that says the important points about your business and let people know how to reach you (WhatsApp, Messages, calls, and website)

Example:

♡ ◯ ◁   🔖

2 likes

dubai.tourss We are Your Best friend in Dubai !
Relax and let us arrange you an unforgettable Trip!

-Book hotels

-Rent a car (low prices)

-Professional Tour guides

-dubai activities

.More info ➡️ Direct message us 🔍

.

17

4

Hashtags Strategy

4- A photo that has a hashtag in its description will automatically be discoverable to anyone who's browsing that hashtag.

Let's talk about a coffee shop example: If you're trying to get coffee lovers into your shop, use hashtags like #localcoffeeshop or #latteart. You can even hashtag the name of your business. Avoid irrelevant hashtags, though. If you can't come up with eleven, don't stress too much. If you add a ton of random hashtags, your photos will end up in front of the wrong people.

Hashtags is how new people can find your page, so use relevant hashtags in the bottom of the caption, but don't be too general, for example; don't use: #fashion, instead use: #abaya or #Menstshirt or anything specific that you would search for to find this product.

Type the hashtag on Instagram and choose the hashtags that suits your account level, because if there's 12 million posts in this hashtag your post as a new page won't compete and won't show.

Example:

#	#travel 620M posts	*Too High*
#	#traveldairies 659K posts	*High*
#	#traveldaily 345K posts	*Good*
#	#traveldairy 101K posts	*Very Good*
#	#traveldaires 32.1K posts	*Good*
#	#traveldairies🩶 5000+ posts	*Too low*

-COMBINE AND TEST Hashtags:

You can try with different hashtags, test them and see which ones give you the best results.

-keywords a customer would search:

You should try to be specific as much as you can. You need to put yourself in the shoes of the buyer.

-how many Hashtags?

I suggest using 8-15 Hashtag per post. (Instagram limit is 30)

GROW IT

Congratulations, now that you have established your business page and made new customers, it's time to grow your business and reach for new audience.

There are some strategies that you can follow and try to see which works best for your business.

Each business is different and some techniques might work with you and some wouldn't.

1

Find customers

Now that your page is ready, it's time for people to see it!

But how will people find you, while you're still new with no followers?

You have to find them!

First, find a business page similar to yours, for example: if you're selling flowers, find local flower shops page, don't go for global pages with millions of followers, the best followers number is between 3k – 50k, cause there audience is more active and real.

Second, follow their followers.

By doing this people who are already interested in your category will check your page to see who followed them, and since you already have all your services and products posted they might go through them and become a customer.

You have to repeat this every day, the more you do it the more customers you might get, but be careful not to overdo it because Instagram might think you are a robot and delete your account.

Tip: if you do this process for few days and didn't get any inquiries or orders, you should try another page, because their followers might not be real or active.

Keep changing pages until you find one that brings you customers.

After a while you need to stop for few days and unfollow these people so you don't reach the maximum limit.

And then you can start following new people again.

- After you gain an amount of followers you should remind them with your services and offers with stories and posts, I will recommend 2-4 days a week, don't be spamming people with the same pictures again and again, and try to come up with different posts even if the idea is the same.

2

Use Stories

Insta-Stories are just as important as the content published on your insta-feed.

They give an authentic and direct connection to your followers and helps them get to know you and your business a lot better.

You can use "Canva" to create eye-catching designs with ready templates!

Want to add animated text to your content? U can try "Legend app" Or "Hype Type" app If you want to create videos with music, add text and animated pictures to your Stories, then play around in "InShot" app (available for both Android and iOS!).

Ideas to post on Stories:

- Tips and tricks related to your business.

- How-To tutorials

-How to use your product

-What's the benefits of your product?

- How your product helped others (Customers Reviews)

For example, if your business sells a product, it could be more beneficial to post videos of real people using your product or "how-to" videos.

-Behind the Scenes

-Launching new products

-Collection Preparations

-Top 10 bestselling products on your website

-top 10 questions about your product

- Q&A or polls

Start a conversation, get feedback from your followers, and ask them anything and everything that interests you

So my first tip for you is to tell a story. It might seem obvious, but you'd be surprised how many brands don't follow this advice or worse – don't know how to use Insta-Stories to tell their story. Your

Instagram strategy shouldn't be just a bunch of randomly picked visuals. All these elements need to play well together to tell a complete story of your business. Let your followers enjoy watching your stories instead of skipping them. Even though Insta Stories are pieces of a puzzle that will disappear in 24 hours, they can still have an impact.

Tip: You can add hashtags to your stories to get discovered by new followers and encourage engagement

And you can add a story set as highlights for new followers to see when they find your page for the first time.

Tip: Highlight covers are just as important as the highlighted stories. Be sure to create an enticing Instagram highlight covers for your highlights, you can google (highlights symbols for Instagram) or design them with Canva.

3

Discounts Strategy

2- you can make offers every 2-3 months, people love a good discount, if they're already following you and are interested in your business, the discount will give them that extra push to buy!

But don't overdo it because you'll burn your original price, and no one would buy except with the discount.

Offers examples:

-Buy 1 Get 1 free

-20% OFF Everything

-Refer a friend and get X

4

Packages Strategy

2- Packages is another thing that people love! because they feel like they're getting more value for a lower price, so make a good package/set and use "Canva" to design a picture for this offer and make sure to write the price on it, with preferably a Red color, because according to researchers the red color causes people to react with greater speed and force which makes them feel the urgent need to take an action.

5

Video content

3-focus on video content, especially REELS.

I'm sure you noticed that video content gets higher interactions and affects the viewer emotions more.

And don't worry you don't need an expensive camera to do that, you can use your phone and still make an awesome video.

Mobile Apps you can use:

-Canva, inshot, legend, hype type, videoleap, tiktok, magisto.

You can use YouTube to get inspired with some ideas to shoot your specific product too.

Tip: if you want good interaction with your posts, don't ever use the landscape size (wither it's videos or pictures), always portrait or square size, because while the user is scrolling through the application, you want to be able to grab his attention in 2-3 seconds, if you don't he'll just skip your post, and in order to do that you need to occupy a big size on his screen.

Example:

As you can see, I'm occupying most of your phone screen while you're scrolling, so I the chances are higher that I might catch your attention to stop and watch.

But here, the picture size is too small, so I need to focus to see the details, and the usual user won't make that effort most of the time.

Not to mention that my eyes can move to the next post cause it's halfway there!

6

Reels is King

Reels, Instagram's short-form, looping video feature, is still one of the most effective ways to reach new audiences on the app.

Reels are the easiest way to go viral on Instagram. The Instagram algorithm loves Reels, and posting them will automatically get you far more visibility and reach.

Unlike most of the Instagram experience, viewers in the Reels feed are served high interest content from both users they follow, and users they don't.

This means the Reels you create can easily reach far beyond your follower list – helping to increase your visibility and grow your follower count.

For the best results:

- Use keywords and hashtags in your Reels captions that

accurately describe your video content

- Use trending sounds, and align the transitions of the video with the audio.

- Catch the eyes of the user in the first 1-3 seconds, if you don't he will just skip you.

- Keep your Reels short and snappy to encourage repeat views

- Surprise people, with anything unexpected, the element of

surprise makes the viewer watch again and mostly interact with you.

- Create original content, you don't have to spend hours filming, but you can create a simple short video that delivers the message.

- Give value, try to give your viewer a useful information, or even a helpful tip, this will make them save the video which will make Instagram see that you have a valuable video and push it to more people to watch.

- Create sharable content, something that you might send to your friend, maybe because it reminded you of them or you saw a valuable information in the video so you share it to benefit them.

- Add on-screen text for viewers watching without sound

- Aim for high-quality video footage (rather than uploading content with a TikTok watermark)

- Call to action, at the end of your video type something like:

  -Details in caption
  -follow for more
  -follow for part 2
  -call to know more
  -give a discount code
  -share with your bestie
  -save for later

By doing this you'll be directing the viewer to consume more of your content and spend more time on your profile which increases your reach and impressions.

Even if your brand or business doesn't feel like an obvious fit for Reels, there are still ways to see success.

Let me give you 22 reels ideas a small business can do:

- o Show Your Work Space
- o Meet My Team
- o Introduce Yourself
- o Let's Make a Product!
- o Share Explainer Videos to Introduce Your Business
- o Work From Home
- o Behind the Scenes
- o Let's Pack Some Orders
- o Unbox Your Products
- o Follow the Trend
- o Answer an FAQ

- How it Started vs. How it's going
- Repurpose Your Posts and Stories
- How-to Videos
- Reality vs. Expectations
- Before and After
- Share Small Tips
- Do What People Ask for in Comments
- Positive Reactions – customer Reviews
- Share the Tools You Use
- Celebrate Your business Birthday
- Recreate a Look Using Your Products

7

Add QR Code

Utilize Your Instagram QR Code to
Increase Followers and brand awareness.

Instagram allows you to have a custom QR code for your profile that you can add to anything you want so people can easily scan it and find you on Instagram.

This code can be placed on your business card, thank you cards placed in order packages, or even on your products as stickers, and boxes used to ship out orders. This allows you to actively promote your Instagram profile offline and online.

How can I get this QR code?

To get your own custom Instagram QR code:

1-Open your Instagram app.

2-Go to your Instagram profile.

3-Press on the three lines icon on top – at the top right corner.

4-You will see "QR Code"

5- Capture it and crop it.

The more you promote your Instagram profile, the more potential customers you can get.

8

Listen to people

Do What People Ask for in comments.

Sometimes they might ask for tutorials, or how do you edit your videos... etc.

Whenever you run out of ideas, ask your followers for some!

Share a story or post and ask your followers what they'd like to see on your next Instagram reels. Now, you'll get tons of messages and comments that give you some fantastic Instagram reels ideas. Pick the ones you find more interesting and save them somewhere to avoid running out of content.

This method really works and helps you get more Instagram engagement under your post and give you new ideas for your upcoming content.

Tip: Whenever you are using one of those followers' ideas, share the original comment on your reels to show your audience that you care about them and read every comment or message.

8

Paid promotion Strategy

4- Pick the best performing post on your page (the one that most people ask questions about and interact with it) and try promoting it on Instagram by paid boosting it, if you don't know how to do that you can YouTube it and follow step by step.

But again don't be too general with choosing audience, for example if you're selling makeup, make sure to choose only females, and choose beauty as their interest. Also for the location, don't choose a whole country, or a city, choose an area if you can, where you know your audience will mostly live there.

8

PR Packages

5-Around 50% of social media users prefer getting product information from their favorite influencers rather than the brand itself.

Influencer marketing gives a higher ROI when it comes to advertisements. Send your products to influencers and celebrities & give them discount codes to know the number of sales coming from them directly.

Micro-influencing in particular is a strong opportunity for brand endorsement. The more followers the influencer has the more chance that they will expect a paid AD not only products, so it's up to you and your budget.

9

Smart Advertising

Think like a customer not as a business owner.

Don't go for the direct marketing all the time; Shop now, buy now, order this...etc.

Instead: think how would they benefit from your product in their life? Or what problem will your product solve for them?

For example: if you have a gift shop page, you can say: when was the last time you got a nice gift for your mom? Or make her day and check out our new gifts collection to pick an awesome gift to surprise her!

10

Post timing

7-Choose the right time to post:

Optimize your posting time to get the most likes and good reach by looking at information Instagram has already provided you with.

You can see your insights if you switch your account to business (in the setting), then press on insights > followers > scroll down > most active times:

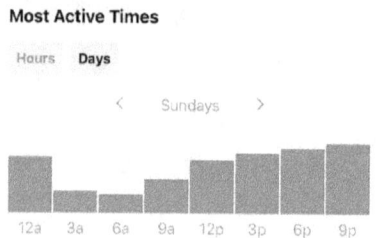

Play with posting times at first, and see what works for you, you should be able to see when to post according to the most likes you get at a given time.

Tip: If you're a B2B business, the best times to post on Instagram are from 12:00 pm to 1:00 pm, Monday through Friday. If you're a B2C business, you should focus your efforts on evenings and weekends.

Tip: use an alarm on your phone to remind you to post on time.

The "Later app" is another great example you can use which, aside from previewing your feed, is also quite handy for scheduling your pictures on Instagram.

11

Giveaways

You can run a giveaway every 2-3 months to gift your audience some of your products or services, in exchange they should follow your business page and invite their friend in the comments to follow you as well.

How to run a "Follow to Enter" Giveaway:

1- Create or use an attractive, engaging photo of your prize (your product is the best way) to grab their attention.

2- Write a clear caption. If you want to have a successful giveaway you need to give your followers clear and precise instructions. Be sure to make the instructions as simple as possible.

Example:

To win ******

1-follow our page

2-like the post

3-mention 3 friends in the comments

(This spreads the image further, increases the number of people that will see it, and achieves more entrants.

This can translate easily to more followers and more likes on your future photos)

4- Pick the winner randomly from the likes, and film it, make sure the winner is following you, then announce it.

Tip: After you pick the winner you can post a picture of the prize and tag them, this will give new people scrolling through your page more reasons to follow.

Tip: you can also reach out to other pages with similar or higher following than you, and arrange more gifts and bigger giveaways.

12

Add Your Location

Adding a location tag to your posts helps
to boost your local engagement and likes

on Instagram. This is because these posts will be made more visible to people in that area.

You can do this by adding local hashtags as we stated in our previous tips or you can add a geo-location to your post.

You can also add your location with an Instagram story sticker as well. This helps your stories to pop in the discovery feed of those nearby or in that exact location.

People looking for photos near them will be likely to engage with them, meaning you have a good chance to get more likes on your photos.

< **New Post** Share

Write a caption...

Tag people >

Tag products >

Add reminder >

Add Location >

Dubai, United Arab Emirates...   Global Village

Boost post

13

Create Instagram Guides

Basically, Instagram Guides are like a combination of carousel posts and blog posts. They allow you to share more information and can be a powerful source for improved Instagram engagement.

Take your viewers in a journey moving from picture to picture, it can be talking about you and your business, or providing new information to benefit your viewers.

Examples:

-How to know your body type

-How to choose outfits for your body type

-5 things makes our product special

-How to know your skin type

-How to order from our website

You can design this guide on Instagram story, or on canva.

And post them as a carousal post, one step at a time.

This can include products, influencers, public figures, brands, and more, that are published on Instagram.

14

Post happy customers

Try to use any good reviews you get from customers, by reposting their pictures using your product, or capturing their messages saying their opinion about it.

But try to put it in a certain design or a theme to match your page colors and aesthetics.

15

Setup Instagram shop

What is Instagram shopping?

Instagram Shopping is a feature that allows ecommerce brands to create a digital, shareable catalog of their products right on Instagram.

An Instagram Shop is a brand's customizable digital storefront, which

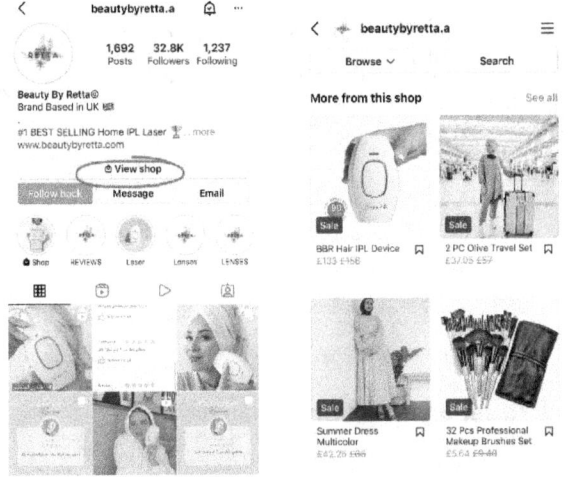

allows customers to shop right from your Instagram profile.

More than 130 million users tap on an Instagram Shopping post each month — foot traffic a shop owner could only dream of.

So if you have products to sell, it's time to set up your virtual storefront. Let's get started.

How to set up Instagram shopping?

Step 1: Convert to a Business or Creator Account

If you don't already have a Business (or Creator) account on Instagram, you have to switch it.

Step 2: Connect To a Facebook Page

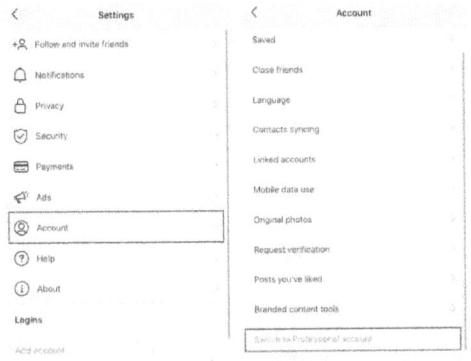

You can't have an Instagram Shop without a Facebook Page, so hopefully you have one already.

1. On Instagram, go to Edit Profile.

2. Under Public Business Information, select Page

3. Choose your Facebook Business Page to connect.

Step 3: Upload your product catalog

Okay, this is the part where you actually upload all of your products. You've got a couple of different options here. You can either input every product manually into Facebook Business manager, or integrate a pre-existing product database from a certified ecommerce platform (like Shopify or BigCommerce.)

For the manual way I will take you step by step on how to do it:

1. Logged into your Facebook Business account, go to Commerce Manager.

2. Click Get Started and select Create a Catalog.

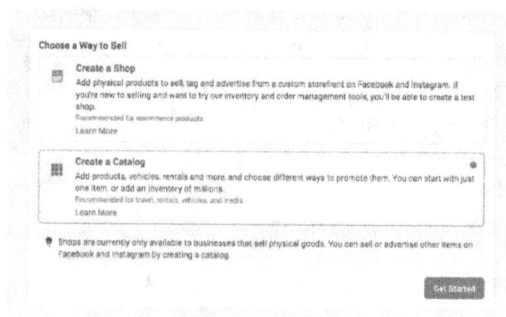

3. Select Ecommerce (products) and click next.

4. Select how you'd like to add items to your catalog: in this case, choose Upload Product Info.

5. Assign this catalog to your Business Manager account.

6. Enter a name for your catalog.

7. Click Create.

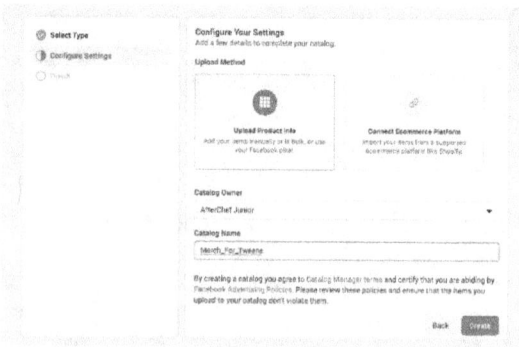

8. Head back to Commerce Manager and select your catalog.

9. Open up the Catalog tab and navigate to Items.

10. Select Add Items, then Add Manually, and hit next.

11. Upload an image of your item — this should be at least 500 x 500 pixels.

12. Enter a name, description, and other details. Get specific so the SEO & google can help shoppers find your great goods.

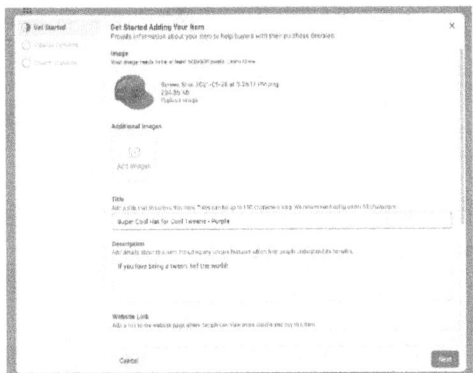

13. In the Item Category section, select your specific category.

14. Under Create Variants, add different sizes or colors if desired.

15. When you're done, click Finish... or hit "Add another Item" and start back at step 12.

That's it!

If you want to automatically import products from a pre-existing website, you can search on YouTube on how to do that for your exact website type.

Step 3: Submit your account for review

At this point, you'll need to submit your account for review. These reviews usually take a couple of days, but sometimes it might run longer.

Step 4: Turn on Instagram Shopping

Once you've passed the account review process, it's time to connect your product catalog with your Instagram Shop.

-Go to your Instagram profile settings.

-Tap Business, then Shopping.

-Select the product catalog you'd like to connect. And you're done!

After setting up your Instagram shop, you can use a Shopping Tag to tag products from your catalog in your Stories, Reels, or Instagram posts, so your audience can click through to learn more or buy, awesome right!

Have patience

Many marketers have common mistake when using Instagram, they only aim to

drive sales but that's not how it works. Using Instagram for business is about building a brand, creating conversation, reaching out towards your customers, engaging with them and inspiring them with your products and services.

Use Instagram as a tool for creating brand awareness through quality and relatable content that your target audience will love.

If you expect your numbers to go up in a month, two or even a year, just because you've started your brand's Instagram account, I must disappoint you – that's not how it works. Your building quality audience, people who are actually interested in your business, so take your time. Post quality photos. Focus on engagement, not on a total number of followers. Work on improving the number of likes on your photos, increasing engagement and comments below the content you post.

Consistency is key

You should keep posting and be active in order for your account to grow, but don't be spammy. No need to post 10 pictures a day. Instead, one or two really good ones might have more influence than these ten. Quality over quantity – always. Be genuine and authentic, but also, be consistent. Don't go too long between posting two photos. A few days is okay – a few weeks is not.

Connect to other social media platforms

For a small business willing to expand through Instagram, connecting apps is excellent.

You can have direct links from your Instagram to your other socials like Facebook, Twitter or Tiktok.

You can even apply everything you learned in this book to other social platforms because you can use the same designs on all of them, this will help you reach a bigger audience.

What's next?

When you start a business, what is your main priority? To have the most sales you can possibly have, right?

Having an online reach for your business is a great way to increase sales but it could be a challenge for less tech-savvy people. Most of us who don't have an IT background won't know how to create a shopping website but I will recommend to you some website builders that will get the job done for you.

If you want to take your business to the next level and showcase your products or services on your own e-commerce website, you have many options available online depending on your needs, but I personally prefer these two:

1-payhip.com

Pros:

-it's free to start.

The best thing about it is that you won't be paying any subscription fees, unlike other ecommerce platforms, Payhip doesn't charge anything upfront.

They only make money when you do, by getting a 5% commission from your sales.

And if you didn't make any, that's totally fine, no charges to pay.

-minimalistic design

It's perfect if you want something simple, easy and give your clients the ability to pay online.

-very easy to use and quick to setup, you can do it in few hours.

-Secure payments.

It doesn't handle payments, it takes customers to the most trusted merchants such as Paypal, Stripe, Visa or Mastercard.

You can connect your PayPal account and receive card payments from your customers worldwide.

- I highly recommend this website if you're selling **services or digital products.**

CONS:

-it's too simple.

Lack of many design features, the customization options available are very basic.

-Support

They're not really responsive if you're facing an issue, but don't worry most of you are not going to face any issues, it's usually easy and smooth platform.

2- Wix or Shopify

Pros:

- All in one platforms.

These two are similar website builders that you can use to develop your website without coding or a website developer.

- Website name.

Another advantage is that you can have your brand name as the website name by purchasing a domain name.

- Fully customizable.

It has so many ready templates that you can pick from and edit it to make it your own.

-Email hosting

Wix supports hosting your own email with shop name, example: info@myshopname.com

But Shopify doesn't have this feature.

Cons:

- paid subscription.

To use one of these two you need to pay subscription fees depending on your package.

If you don't subscribe to any package, Ads will be showing on your website.

- Many features

You should YouTube the difference between Wix and Shopify to choose the one that suits your needs best.

Do your research to find the right option for you.

That's all. Follow these steps to grow your brand and become a visible face on every social media platform.

If you have benefited from the strategies in this book please share your review with us and recommend it to your friends.

Wish you all the happiness and success.

@retta.a